THE WORLD AROUND US

ON OUR NATURE WALK

Our First Talk About Our Impact on the Environment

Dr. Jillian Roberts
Foreword by Bob McDonald

Illustrations by Jane Heinrichs

ORCA BOOK PUBLISHERS

I dedicate this book to all the teachers around the world who have dedicated their lives to the education of children. Children are our most precious resource!
—JR

For my daughter, who inspires me every day with her love of nature.
—JH

Library and Archives Canada Cataloguing in Publication

Title: On our nature walk : our first talk about our impact on the environment / Dr. Jillian Roberts ; foreword by Bob McDonald ; illustrations by Jane Heinrichs.
Names: Roberts, Jillian, 1971- author. | Heinrichs, Jane, 1982- illustrator.
Series: World around us (Orca Book Publishers)
Description: Series statement: The world around us
Identifiers: Canadiana (print) 20190172142 | Canadiana (ebook) 20190172150 |
ISBN 9781459821002 (hardcover) |
ISBN 9781459821019 (PDF) | ISBN 9781459821026 (EPUB)
Subjects: LCSH: Nature—Effect of human beings on—Juvenile literature. |
LCSH: Human ecology—Juvenile literature.
Classification: LCC GF75 .R63 2020 | DDC J304.2—DC23

Summary: Young readers are introduced to environmental issues in their own neighborhoods in this illustrated nonfiction picture book.

Library of Congress Control Number: 2019943979
Simultaneously published in Canada and the United States in 2020

Orca Book Publishers is committed to reducing the consumption of nonrenewable resources in the making of our books. We make every effort to use materials that support a sustainable future.

Orca Book Publishers gratefully acknowledges the support for its publishing programs provided by the following agencies: the Government of Canada through the Canada Book Fund and the Canada Council for the Arts, and the Province of British Columbia through the BC Arts Council and the Book Publishing Tax Credit.

Cover and interior art by Jane Heinrichs
Artwork created using English watercolor and Japanese brush pens on Italian watercolor paper.
Design by Rachel Page

Front cover photos: iStock.com (left to right): FatCamera, rawpixel, HRAUN
Back cover photos: iStock.com (left to right): FatCamera, stockstudioX, FatCamera
Interior photos:
iStock.com: © Imgorthand pp. 4, 5, Valdas Jarutis p. 6, Selçuk KARABIYIK p. 7, ElsvanderGun p. 8, VichienPetchmai p. 10, ablokhin p. 11, Nikada p. 12, Wenjie Dong p. 13, Peter Horrox p. 14, PeskyMonkey p. 15, stockstudioX p. 16, FatCamera p. 17, FatCamera p. 22, fstop123 p. 23, xavierarnau, p. 24, FatCamera p. 25, Brasil2 p. 26
Shutterstock.com: © Olga Gorevan p. 9, Dmytro Zinkevych p. 20, chaiviewfinder p. 18, p. 28, Liv Oeian p. 25
Stocksy.com: © Raymond Forbes LLC p. 19, Léa Jones p. 27
Dreamstime.com: © Sjors737 p. 21

ORCA BOOK PUBLISHERS
orcabook.com

Printed and bound in South Korea.

23 22 21 20 • 4 3 2 1

There is no place like Earth. Really!

Scientists have sent robots to every planet in our solar system and found thousands of other planets going around stars in our galaxy. And while all of them are interesting, none of them are like our home world.

Some, like Mercury and Venus, are too hot for humans to visit. Others, such as Jupiter, Saturn, Uranus and Neptune, are giant balls of gas. We would sink into them and be crushed to death by enormous pressure. Even Mars, which is most like Earth, is a cold, dry, desert world with no oxygen in the atmosphere. If you were to visit Mars, you would find living difficult and dangerous, and you would need to wear a spacesuit every time you went outside.

Similar dangers exist on all the other planets found so far. They are interesting but not like Earth. The search is on for another Earth-like planet, and there is a good chance one will be found somewhere out there. But it will be very, very far away from here—too far for our spaceships to reach in a human lifetime. That means Earth is still the only planet we know of where we can step outside and breathe fresh air, feel the wind in our faces, swim in lakes and see other creatures that share the world with us—and do it all without wearing spacesuits.

Earth is our safe home in a deadly universe. It is important that we look after it so we will always have fresh air, clean water and healthy land. It's not too hard to do that. All we need to do is clean up after ourselves and make sure everyone else does the same. After all, it's the only planet we have!

—Bob McDonald, Host of CBC Radio's *Quirks & Quarks*

Today my class went on a walk through the forest to learn about nature. Our teacher said it's important for kids to spend time outside. Why?

Making friends, playing outside and getting exercise are important for everyone's physical and mental health. When we spend time in nature, it makes us feel happier. It does good things for our bodies, like improving our ability to remember things and helping us think more clearly. Also, when we spend time outside, we grow our love and appreciation for nature and our environment.

"Did you know there is really only one ocean on planet Earth, because all the oceans join with each other? This means that anything thrown into the water could potentially circle the globe. That's why debris from the tsunami in Japan is still washing up on the beaches of the west coast of North America. The same is true of pollution. The ocean may carry it out of sight, but it will show up on someone else's shore eventually. There is also only one atmosphere and one biosphere— the web of life. Understanding the interconnectedness is understanding our planet, and that is what science does. The next time you go on a nature walk, pay close attention and be aware of the interconnectedness around you. A nature walk can be almost anywhere—on the beach, in the forest or in your neighborhood park!"

—Bob McDonald

It looked like some people didn't clean up after themselves when they were here. They left garbage on the path. It's wrong to litter. Why did they do that?

Even though many of us were taught not to throw garbage on the ground, some people still do it. Maybe nobody explained to those people how harmful litter is to the environment. Picking up after yourself is a habit—like keeping your room or desk tidy.

Littering is when someone leaves their garbage lying around outside. Usually people litter because they don't understand the consequences of doing it, or they think someone else will clean up after them. But littering can harm wildlife and people, and contaminate water systems and other natural habitats. It is a major cause of some of the critical environmental problems facing our planet.

Sometimes when I go to the beach, I see really big pieces of garbage. How would all that stuff get there?

Sometimes things fall off boats and wash up on the shore with the tides. Litter of any size is bad for the plants and animals that live in and around the ocean, and it can even affect the environments of faraway places. Litter is a form of pollution.

There is a spiral of currents in the North Pacific Ocean that has created a massive collection of trash known as the Great Pacific Garbage Patch. This garbage floats between the west coast of North America and Japan. Some of the garbage is from vessels, but much of it originates on land, and much of it is plastics. These plastics break down into tinier pieces of plastic, called microplastics, which will never fully break down or disappear, and which can kill wildlife.

Are there other kinds of pollution besides garbage?

Pollution comes in many forms. Sometimes pollution is invisible, but whether we see it or not, it can harm animals, people and plants. Air pollution occurs when harmful chemicals and gases are released into the air. Land pollution is when waste or garbage is deposited on the land. Water pollution is when materials contaminate the water. Thermal pollution is when the overall temperature of a body of water changes, which harms fish and other organisms. The constant sound of traffic, construction and other activities in cities creates noise pollution. And excessive or obtrusive lighting creates light pollution, which can damage wildlife cycles and human health.

Yes. Lots of things we do and use in our daily lives contribute to pollution. The exhaust from gas-fueled vehicles and jet-fueled airplanes pollutes the air, for example. The process of making clothes and buildings can release chemicals that pollute the air, the soil and even water systems.

And as the world's population increases, so does the pollution we humans create, as our need for things like energy, water and food grows.

How do more people and more needs affect the environment?

Just as our bodies need food, water and fresh air to survive, our planet needs a balance of air, water, plants, animals and people to be healthy. When we take too many of the earth's resources, or destroy too many natural environments to build areas for humans to live and work in, we upset that balance. This harms the health of the planet and everyone who depends on it for survival.

Natural resources are things we use that come from the natural environment, such as air, water, wood and fossil fuels like coal, oil and natural gas. There are two types of natural resources: renewable and nonrenewable. Renewable resources are in endless supply—for example, air, sunlight and wind. Nonrenewable resources are in limited supply—they will eventually run out. Fossil fuels are nonrenewable resources.

What happens if we don't find that balance?

The planet as we know it will change. There is only one planet Earth, and many of its resources will not last if we keep using them the way we have been. The truth is, right now we aren't doing a very good job of taking care of our planet.

We must be responsible about the products we consume and the things we do so that we can support humans, animals and our natural environments well into the future. This is what's known as sustainability. Our actions will have lasting, significant impacts and consequences that will affect generations to come. We can create a sustainable world by limiting our consumption of materials, protecting our natural environments and finding eco-friendly ways to consume resources.

I feel sad about that, like I'm not doing a good job of taking care of our planet.

The Iroquois, or Haudenosaunee, have a belief that we should make decisions today that will benefit people seven generations into the future (about 140 years). This concept is called the Great Law of the Iroquois, or the Seventh Generation Principle. So next time you are about to throw something in the trash that could be recycled, or you're about to leave the lights on in your house, ask yourself, How may this affect people seven generations from now?

I do too. The earth is a special place, and we all have a responsibility to do everything we can to protect it, for ourselves and for the people who will live here after us— our children, their children, their children's children and so on. Always look for ways to reduce what you use, reuse the things you have and recycle whatever you can't use anymore.

Is anybody doing anything to help our environment?

Yes! Many countries around the world have agreed to work together to help preserve the earth. There are international agreements and laws within countries, states or provinces, and cities to help make sure we are taking better care of our environment.

And lots of scientists, entrepreneurs, activists and kids just like you are doing what they can to help our planet.

The PARIS AGREEMENT is an agreement within the United Nations Framework Convention on Climate Change (UNFCCC) on how to respond to climate change. A primary goal is to keep the rise in global temperature this century to well below 2°C (35.6°F) and to reduce it even further, in the future, to 1.5°C (34.7°F). As of June 2019, 195 countries around the world had signed the agreement, which means they have promised to reduce their carbon dioxide emissions over time.

What can I do
to help?

You can do a lot to protect your environment and help your community at the same time! You could start a cleanup club to deal with litter near your school or in your neighborhood. You could keep a bag in your backpack and pick up trash you see when you are out for a walk with your family (wear reusable gloves, and make sure you don't pick up anything that looks sharp—it could be dangerous). You can even suggest to your teacher that the students in your class each bring a garbage bag along on every field trip!

Community & Environmental Tips for Kids

- Start an art club at your school and use recycled materials.

- Grow your own vegetable garden—ask a grown-up to help you.

- Walk or ride your bike to school if you can.

- Unplug your electronics when you aren't using them, and turn off the lights when you leave a room.

- When you have picnics with your family, pack food in reusable jars and containers.

- Give gently used books instead of goodie bags at your next birthday party.

But I'm just one kid.
How can I make a big
difference?

You may be just one kid, but you've got something special that is unique to you: your imagination. Many of the world's biggest problems have been solved by people who used their imaginations to figure out solutions. Just asking questions about what you see around you is a great start!

Meet Greta Thunberg

Even kids can change the world! Greta Thunberg is a Swedish climate activist who has taken the world by storm. Frustrated with the lack of action taken by adults, Greta decided to take matters into her own hands. She began to skip school on Fridays and protest for climate action outside the Swedish parliament buildings. Her initiative grew into international initiative, whereby school kids from around the world organized school strikes for climate on Fridays. Greta's contribution to raise awareness about climate change garnered her a nomination for the Nobel Peace Prize.

How can an imaginary idea fix a real problem?

Meet Ann Makosinski

Ann is a student, inventor and social entrepreneur who grew up in Victoria, BC. She started participating in science fairs in the sixth grade. In the tenth grade, inspired by a friend in the Philippines who had no electricity for light to study by at nighttime, she invented the Hollow Flashlight. This is no ordinary flashlight—it is powered by the body heat of the human hand! Just by holding the flashlight, you are charging it. Amazing! And because it doesn't need batteries, there are no batteries to recycle.

By innovation. Innovation means using your imagination to think of a better way to do something, and then creating and putting your innovation to the test. And kids are great innovators! The next time you see a problem in the world around you, imagine how you could solve it. Who knows—you might come up with the next great invention!

How can I become someone who innovates?

The best way to get your imagination going is to spend lots of time playing outside, exploring your community and asking lots of questions about the world around you. Take a moment to think about what you see when you go on a nature walk with your school. Are there problems you can help fix? Are there friends and family who would help you? Brainstorm ideas on your own and with others to see what you can come up with. Then choose one idea you're passionate about and get started! There are always new ways to solve problems and work together to protect our environment and all the humans and animals who live in it.

Meet some more people who have used their imaginations to help clean up our world!

The Wavestar machine was initially thought up by Danish brothers and innovators Niels and Keld Hansen, who came up with the concept in 2000 after being inspired by their love of water. The Wavestar machine converts kinetic wave power into electricity. This technology has been evolving for over a decade. This innovative machine sits in the water with special floats that harvest the energy of waves, similar to how windmills capture energy. The scientists at Wavestar believe that we will need diverse sources of unlimited clean energy to meet the energy needs of the 21st century. Long gone are the days when we could rely on fossil fuels. I wonder how many other cool ideas will be shared in the years to come!

Deepika Kurup is a young scientist, speaker, social entrepreneur and student at Harvard University. Deepika has been passionate about solving the global water crisis since she was in middle school. What sparked her passion was seeing children in India drinking dirty and contaminated water. Over the next few years she researched and developed a simpler and more cost-effective water-purification system using solar energy (energy from the sun) to help remove contaminants from drinking water.

Param Jaggi is an American inventor and social entrepreneur. When he was 15, Param invented the EcoTube, a device that can be clipped onto the exhaust pipe of a car, which is where carbon dioxide is emitted. The device passes the carbon dioxide through live algae and converts it to oxygen and sugar. His invention reduces carbon dioxide emissions by 50 percent.

A Note from Dr. Jillian Roberts, Author and Child Psychologist

When we launched the World Around Us series, we quoted Google's Education Evangelist Jaime Casap, who said: "Don't ask kids what they want to be when they grow up, but what problems they want to solve." Protecting our environment is one of the most pressing problems our world is facing today. I challenge all the readers of this book to try to solve the environmental problems in their particular corner of the world. Sometimes little solutions can inspire bigger solutions. We are all part of the interconnectedness of nature, and the world needs our collective problem-solving innovations. Perhaps you will be inspired to solve an environmental problem the next time you go on a nature walk!

Resources

Print

Bergen, Lara. *Don't Throw That Away!* New York: Little Simon, 2009.

Brown, Peter. *The Wild Robot.* New York: Little, Brown and Company, 2016.

Hopkins, H. Joseph. *The Tree Lady: The True Story of How One Tree-Loving Woman Changed a City Forever.* San Diego: Beach Lane Books, 2013.

Kaye, Cathryn Berger. *A Kids' Guide to Climate Change & Global Warming: How to Take Action!* Minneapolis: Free Spirit, 2009.

McAnulty, Stacy. *Earth!: My First 4.54 Billion Years.* New York: Henry Holt, 2017.

Nivola, Claire. *Life in the Ocean: The Story of Oceanographer Sylvia Earle.* New York: Farrar, Straus and Giroux, 2012.

Paul, Miranda. *One Plastic Bag: Isatou Ceesay and the Recycling Women of Gambia.* Minneapolis: Millbrook Press, 2015.

Thornhill, Jan. *The Tragic Tale of the Great Auk.* Toronto: Groundwood Books, 2016.

Online

Earth Rangers: earthrangers.com/

EcoKids: earthday.ca/ecokids/

Garbology: naturebridge.org/garbology.php

Mazu—Social Media with Manners: mazufamily.com

National Geographic Kids: kids.nationalgeographic.com/

National Wildlife Federation—Ranger Rick: rangerrick.org/

Links to external resources are for personal and/or educational use only and are provided in good faith without any express or implied warranty. There is no guarantee given as to the accuracy or currency of any individual item. Orca Book Publishers provides links as a service to readers. This does not imply any endorsement by Orca Book Publishers of any of the content accessed through these links.

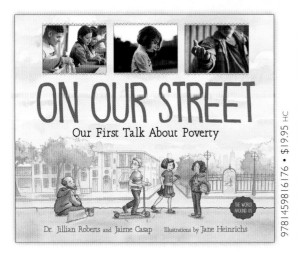

ON OUR STREET
Our First Talk About Poverty

9781459816176 • $19.95 HC

Dr. Jillian Roberts and Jaime Casap   Illustrations by Jane Heinrichs

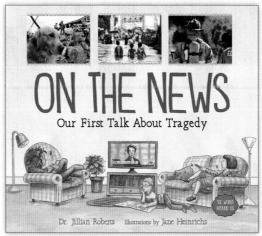

ON THE NEWS
Our First Talk About Tragedy

9781459817845 • $19.95 HC

Dr. Jillian Roberts   Illustrations by Jane Heinrichs

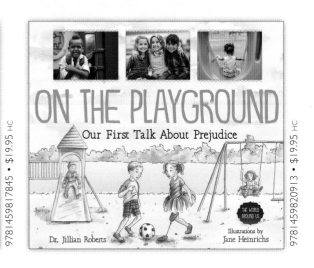

ON THE PLAYGROUND
Our First Talk About Prejudice

9781459820913 • $19.95 HC

Dr. Jillian Roberts   Illustrations by Jane Heinrichs

ON THE INTERNET
Our First Talk About Online Safety

9781459820944 • $19.95 HC

Dr. Jillian Roberts   Illustrations by Jane Heinrichs

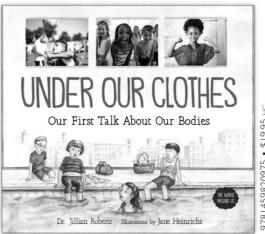

UNDER OUR CLOTHES
Our First Talk About Our Bodies

9781459820975 • $19.95 HC

Dr. Jillian Roberts   Illustrations by Jane Heinrichs

These inquiry-based books are an excellent cross-curricular resource encouraging children to explore and discuss important issues and **foster their own compassion and empathy.**

AGES 6–8 • 32 PAGES
FULL-COLOR PHOTOGRAPHS • RESOURCES INCLUDED

TheWorldAroundUsSeries.com